THE $500, 000 BLUEPRINT

The Beginners' Guide to Making
Money Online Non-Stop Even While
You Sleep

GODWINS INKLINE

THE $500, 000 BLUEPRINT

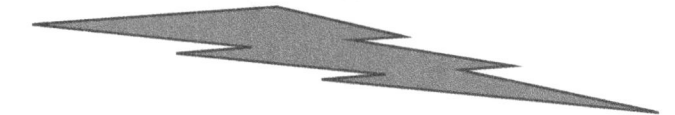

Dedicated to every online entrepreneur resiliently and strategically offering their services.

Copyright

No part of this book is allowed to be reproduced in any form without approval from the author.

Other books by the author:

The $3,000 Blueprint

Online Passive Income

Table of Content

CHAPTER 1

Cultivating Abundance and Prosperity Thinking

Think for a moment. Push away the doubts. Silence the cynic and the inner critic. Let your imagination soar as you envision the kind of existence you'd craft if you suddenly had more wealth, resources, and time freedom than you knew what to do with.

What does that reality look, feel, taste like? What are you most thrilled to begin, try, give, explore? Don't censure or limit yourself. Let your vision be expansive, vivid, and rich. By applying diligently the secrets that will be reviewed in this book, you'd be counting at least $500,000 in your account in the next six months.

Now, this is key: Hold that vision and feeling for as long as you can. Let it infuse your mind and body, like water nourishing a seedling until leaves unfurl in lush abundance. This is the essence of prosperity thinking—getting in deep touch with what abundance truly means and feels like to you, individually. Just like personal empowerment, abundance is an inside job, unique to your values and what "wealth" means to you. And it must first be imaginatively experienced and felt so your subconscious can get to work bringing it to fruition.

It's time to break the pattern of scarcity mindset that's so insidiously pervasive in our culture. We pinball between worry about our own finances and guilt over the world's pressing needs. But true abundance doesn't come from grasping and hoarding. It comes from Imagining, Generating, Multiplying, and Sharing. As your wealth grows, so grows your ability to fund the projects and solutions you care about. Scarcity slows progress; Abundance accelerates it exponentially. Our world needs more people daring to prosper, then paying it forward.

You have everything you need, right now in this moment, to begin to generate abundance. Close your eyes once more. Envision, feel, and let thriving be cultivated from within, then spill forth in manifold ways into your reality. A billion green beings burst forth from tiny seeds no larger than grains of sand. What will you now sprout, grow, and give forth?

Goal-Setting and Vision Boards

As the Cheshire Cat told a perplexed Alice, "If you don't know where you are going, any road will get you there." We've all experienced that feeling of wandering aimlessly, as days bleed into months and even years with little meaningful progress. Goal-setting gives us a destination and vision boards help crystallize the path to get there.

The science is clear that if you don't consciously define your dreams, you're unlikely to realize them. In a study on new graduates pursuing arts careers, 70% of those who didn't set goals had failed to find work after two years. Of those who did set concrete goals, an impressive 95% were employed full-time in their field within one year of graduation. Setting SMART goals works.

SMART is an acronym for:

Specific – Clearly define what, where, when, how much

Measurable – Include metrics to track progress

Achievable – Within realistic scope and abilities

Relevant – Tied directly to what matters most

Time-bound – With set deadlines to create accountability

Now a vision board takes this process further, utilizing our brains' exceptional visual processing abilities to imprint the end goal more concretely. Studies performed at universities including Harvard demonstrated that information coded both verbally and visually activates more neurological pathways, leading to a better memory imprint. Athletes have utilized vision boards for decades and research reveals over 90% achieve most images manifested.

Follow this step-by-step guide to create your own vision board for success:

1. Set aside at least one hour without distractions in an inspirational space. Play empowering music. Begin by relaxing and clearing your mind as best you can of stress or limiting beliefs.

2. On a large poster board or digitally, arrange an affirmation such as "My dreams manifest easily" or "Anything I can conceive & believe, I can achieve" at the center.

3. Mine magazines and websites for visually resonant images and words representing your goals – don't overthink or edit yourself. Print or clip them out as you're drawn to each one. Categories may include dream house, lifestyle

perks, family trips, dream job title, creative passions pursued or community service.

4. Arrange images, quotes & other elements intuitively on your board, adjusting until you LOVE what you see and how it makes you feel looking at this snapshot representing the attainment of your most precious dreams and goals already manifested.

5. Finally and most crucially, spend at least 5-10 minutes daily visualizing this board, immersing your emotional and sensory being into this alternate reality as vividly as possible. Neurologically imprint this completed vision as already achieved. Use it as a touchstone when doubts creep in.

The universe often manifests what we dwell upon, since that is the energetic vibration we emit. Wander without intentional goals and you may end up anywhere. But harness the exceptional power of the human brain to conceptualize, create and manifest the specific reality you envision for yourself. Then determinedly take step-by-step actions each day to get there. With vision boards as your guide and goals as your compass, those once-hazy dreams become sharply visible on the horizon. And soon you'll find yourself not just glimpsing, but inhabiting them fully at last – the life you've dared to dream now gloriously tangible and real all around you.

Managing Limiting Beliefs

Mark Twain once quipped, "It ain't what you don't know that gets you into trouble. It's what you know for sure that just ain't so." Unfortunately, so much of what we "know" to be true about ourselves and what's possible for our lives stems from faulty core beliefs. These become self-fulfilling prophecies that manifest the very mediocrity or failure we hoped to avoid. Challenging limiting beliefs takes mindfulness, courage and persistence, but doing so can unfetter us to pursue our highest potentials.

Common limiting beliefs include:

- I'm not smart/talented enough to succeed at X
- I don't deserve abundance/happiness
- Taking risks leads to failure
- If it seems too good to be true, it is
- I'm too old/young/inexperienced/overcommitted...

We absorb notions like this from early childhood experiences and media messaging. They operate silently as mental scripts running on autopilot, informing our expectations and actions without conscious thought. Stanford psychologist Carol Dweck calls these a "fixed mindset" as opposed to a flexible, learning-oriented "growth mindset." Fixed beliefs trigger fear and avoidance; growth mindsets encourage experimentation, learning from failure and achievement.

It takes mindful presence to notice limiting beliefs when they arise as doubts, hesitation, or thoughts of being undeserving. Strategies like journalling, meditation and openly discussing them help bring them into conscious awareness. Next, begin questioning their factuality. When did you adopt this notion as truth? Does compelling evidence support it? Or have there been exceptions you've dismissed? This builds motivation for change.

Now do some belief experimentation. Temporarily adopt an opposing belief - what some psychologists call "acting as-if." Monitor your decisions, emotions and experiences over the next week living under this new belief, taking note of any shifts. Collect real-world data to test restrictive notions. Seek examples of those actually achieving what your limiting belief deems impossible. This expands perceived options by exposing flaws in absolute, generalized thinking.

Also pay attention to belief phrasing. Words manifest. "Wanting" casts us as lacking. "Hoping to..." keeps achievement at arm's length indefinitely. Shift statements to affirmatively declare goals reached. Repeat revised beliefs aloud. Post them prominently. The brain can be rewired surprisingly quickly with repetition of new neural pathways.

Recruit your subconscious ally through visualization. Athletes have utilized this strategy for decades to improve performance by repeatedly envisioning goals as already accomplished, cementing the experience neurologically before physically actualizing it through practice. Use vision boards, journals or recordings to immerse yourself in sensory details of achievements defying your limiting beliefs. Programming the subconscious primes it to recognize and seize opportunities aligning with your growth-oriented beliefs.

Stay alert for backsliding and self-doubt. Our minds default to comfortable old pathways without diligent upkeep. Review early warning signs like hesitation or eroding enthusiasm. Quickly reroute your inner dialogue before stories power into runaway trains.

Be your own cheerleader. Celebrate small wins that provide evidence against limiting beliefs.

Above all, manifest compassion for the flawed inner narrator attempting to protect you based on outdated information or painful past experiences. We all carry these scars. But now with mindful presence and determination, you can heal them. Write a new story for your life – it's yours for the authoring. It is obvious this process takes patience and perseverance, but freedom from self-imposed constraints is well worth the journey. Recommit each morning: you've got this! And soon that once-powerful inner saboteur loses its grip, freeing you at last to build the full, rich potential that's been inside you all along.

CHAPTER 2

Making Money from Home

Getting Started With Dropshipping

Have you ever dreamed of running your own online business selling interesting products or designs, but lacked the upfront funds for manufacturing inventory? Or perhaps you love seeking out unique gift items or apparel but cringe at the risks retailers take on, especially new entrepreneurs. There is an elegant solution growing ever more popular: dropshipping. This retail method allows anyone to run an independent ecommerce store with no money down on inventory.

Here's how simple dropshipping works: the store owner builds a shopping website showcasing products often sourced from a wholesale supplier directory. When an order comes in, the payment goes to your account. You then place a matching order with the supplier and provide their shipping destination. Presto! The factory sends off the item on your behalf straight to the eager customer's doorstep.

For new ecommerce entrepreneurs, dropshipping offers an invaluable low-risk entry point to assess product-market fit without heavy upfront investment in inventory that may prove stagnant. It can also take customer service headaches off your plate if the manufacturer handles returns or issues. Now globalized supply chains feature factory-direct wholesale pricing that allows sufficient margin for retailers to build in markup. Simultaneously, small manufacturing operations keep sprouting up offering specialized or hand-crafted goods. This convergence sets the stage for a golden age of micro ecommerce entrepreneurs.

Nimble niche websites can drive organic traffic through SEO and social media leveraging the long tail of narrow interests virtually untapped by big box retailers. Ever searched for the perfect gift like Star

Trek uniform onesies for your niece's imminent arrival but came up empty at Target? Such enthusiasts' online meccas thrive on dropshipped goods tailored to serve below mass market radar. Food allergy sufferers, hobby fanatics, arts communities and sustainability advocates all congregate around specialized retailers speaking their language. Build that unique digital gathering space filled with hard-to-find objects of desire, and eager followers will come.

Now, dropshipping isn't free money without effort. You'll need to master basics like search-optimized sites, payment systems, marketing channels to build visibility, branding, great product photo aesthetics, compelling copywriting, analytics tracking, plus streamlined fulfillment and customer support processes. The good news? Abundant free educational resources abound, from handy guides on Shopify's robust academy to Youtube tutorials by successful "momtrepreneurs" happy to explain it all while showing off their kids' college funds earned through savvy selling.

Start slowly with low-cost experiments, tweaking product selection using data not hunches until you hone a winning formula. Be Walmart's opposite – limber and niche, highly responsive to unique customer groups wholly underserved in the mass marketplace. Align offerings to burgeoning buyer values like small batch origin, sustainability, inclusive sizing, or determination to support minority-owned makers. Tell their stories authentically. The internet allows even tiny startups to gain loyal followers across oceans so long as you speak powerfully to an emotional need or aspiration currently overlooked.

Yes, competition is abundant but so is eager demand from values-driven shoppers. With a bit of grit, creativity and mindfulness to perceive gaps in the market, entrance barriers are remarkably low. And remember, Jeff Bezos started off selling books from his garage through a fledgling thing called "the internet" back when the concept seemed unfathomably risky. Dropshipping marks the modern equivalent - allowing budding entrepreneurs to dip toes into ecommerce at minimal risk before diving all in. Give your dream shop a chance to flourish, one curated niche product at a time.

Monetizing a Blog Or Youtube Channel

You started that blog or YouTube channel as a passion project. Maybe you hoped to connect with others who share your interests, process personal experiences, showcase creative pursuits, or boost professional visibility. Then you realized your site keeps steadily gaining loyal followers. Could channeling that momentum into income allow you to devote more time doing what you love? Absolutely -

with intention and savvy strategies! Welcome to content creator entrepreneurship in the digital era.

Getting started generating income from sites requires learning two skillsets: 1) Producing high-value content consistently and 2) Converting site visitors into paying subscribers, customers or brand partners. Let's explore top ways to monetize through both avenues:

Compelling Content Strategies

Quality and consistency are key for building trusting tribes of returning visitors. Niche focus areas that tap universal human fascinations like humor, food, travel, relationships, money, spirituality or creativity tend to gain traction more quickly in saturated digital seas. Hook attention with shareable titles and images, then overdeliver value.

Leverage formats matching your skills like viral recipe videos, painfully funny comics, witty listicles, astrology explainers, couples' vlogs with relatable dynamics demonstrated, musician gear try-ons and original song debuts. Dig deep on developing mastery around a niche knowledge base audiences crave but find scarce consolidated wisdom about elsewhere online. People willingly pay for expertise that addresses urgent needs or passionate curiosities in accessible ways that feel akin to enjoying conversations with a friend.

Monetization Methods

Once you establish consistent traffic, employ diverse revenue streams for income security through fluctuations. Some monetization options suit certain site types better, so experiment to discover your golden revenue recipe.

Advertising – From display to video ads to sponsorships, media advertising opportunities abound once you hit viewership benchmarks. Adsense by Google provides set-it-and-forget-it automated display ad units. More intimate and integrated sponsor relationships often prove most profitable long-term at modest traffic levels. Choose brands strategically aligned around shared values and content themes. Ensure sponsored posts maintain usual quality and authenticity.

Affiliate Links – Insert curated recommendations for products or services you sincerely use and endorse. The retailer rewards your third party stamp of credibility with commissions on ensuing sales. Successful niches like gear recommendations or deal hunting likely find this method profitable with conversion savvy messaging.

Memberships/Subscriptions – Offering exclusive content, community access and direct interface incentives converts true superfans happy to pay for VIP treatment. Set subscription rates based on production expenses and perceived value. Successful YouTubers lure fans to join exclusive channels. Bloggers offer private discussion groups or special content libraries. Podcast hosts provide early episode access without ads.

Online Courses/Ebooks – Convert your expertise into packaged education products students value enough for purchase. Udemy's platform makes listing video course series simple. Self-publish ebooks through Kindle Direct Publishing. Fitness bloggers offer customized workout and nutrition plans. Photoshop aficionados teach post-production mastery through premium workshops.

Services/Merch – Some niche creators directly offer specialized services like photography shoots, graphic design creation, care packages of gear-tested treats or personally crafted arts and crafts. Custom merch stores turn fans into brand ambassadors sporting channel swag.

The integration possibilities are endless. Try varied income stream additions judiciously without overextending production capacity or diluting content quality and visitor experience. Set targets balancing both income and audience size goals. Stay adaptable, but remain authentic in voice rather than chasing quick clicks through hyper trend-jacking. Value loyal community over millions of disengaged peepers. And remember to enjoy the process – with that quality infused in your brand's DNA, monetization success is sure to follow!

Creating Online Courses Or Membership Sites

In the digital age, expanding avenues now exist to generate income beyond strictly trading hours for dollars. While traditional jobs still dominate most incomes, creative entrepreneurs are increasingly leveraging platforms to profit from packaged expertise through online courses and membership sites.

These autoincome sources sell access to valuable education and community you structure once, then continuously collect proceeds as new students enroll on demand. Like books earning royalties for authors long after writing finishes, well-crafted digital education products can seed passive profits for years while you move on to other projects.

Let's explore critical ingredients for successfully creating and monetizing online courses or member sites:

Narrow Your Niche

Select learning topics showing clear audience demand, but with few robust offerings existing already. Broad fields like "business" or "photography" prove oversaturated. Instead identify targeted needs wanting coverage like "food truck accounting" or "surf photography workflows."

Outline Specific Learning Objectives

Clarify exactly what skills or knowledge students will gain to solve struggles or make progress. Design course modules and materials deliberately to fulfill these concrete objectives. These form your promise to members.

Add Value Through Multimedia Formats

Combine written guides or slide lessons with value-boosting elements like worksheets, audio interviews with experts, interactive quizzes, video tutorials demonstrating techniques, peer discussion groups, or templates to utilize learnings.

Polish Presentation

Recording video or audio lessons requires quality equipment and environments to engage versus distract. Use clear outlines ensuring content stays well-organized and on topic. Edit mercilessly until only high-value content remains.

Incentivize Enrollment

Offer free downloadable samples like a course introduction video or first class. Give past students coupons to share. Consider bundle deals, payment plans or launch discounts to motivate signups. Promote through your website, social channels and niche partners open to cross-promotions.

Simplify Student Access

Upload your course onto platforms like Teachable, Thinkific or Podia specializing in marketing online education. Their gorgeous sales interfaces and seamless purchase / enrollment experiences boost credibility while handling logistics like payment processing, coupons and email automation.

Cultivate Community

Isolation sabotages completion rates. Foster connective elements like rapid instructor responses to questions, regular live video Q&As, focused message boards or meetup groups, and discussion prompts in course materials. Human support systems boost persistence.

Refine Repeatedly

Savvy creators A/B test pricing models, sales page copy, and course structures across cohorts to discover ideal conversion and completion formulas. Analyze interactions and feedback to pinpoint where learners struggle. Continue improving until satisfaction metrics peak through word-of-mouth buzz.

Diversify Passive Income Streams

Online courses provide excellent core products to amplify through other autoincome models like membership communities with tiered access, coaching and consulting add-ons, related book publishing, affiliate promotions, downloadable tools or templates, and more.

The internet dramatically democratized access to education and mentorship. By packaging your expertise into online learning experiences creatively bridging geographic divides, you can support motivated students anywhere while earning passive income from hours invested upfront.

Automate the revenue flow, then enroll new cohorts infinitely. Set alerts when course content needs updating, but otherwise rest easy knowing each new member enrolled earns you cash while you sleep. That's scalable impact and income combined - the ultimate dream for knowledge entrepreneurs converting digital platforms into amplifiers of expertise, service and security.

CHAPTER 3

Investing for Compound Growth

Index fund investing basics

What if there were a way to invest for the long haul by putting money in one basket that tracks the broader market rather than trying to pick individual stocks?

That's the idea behind index fund investing. Index funds provides a low-fee, lower risk way to gain market returns over time without requiring deep experience analyzing industries and individual companies. They offer a great starting point for beginner investors while also making up key holdings even for savvy veterans.

Here are the basics on how index funds work and core reasons to consider index funds in your portfolio:

What is an Index Fund?

Index funds aim to mimic overall market returns rather than beat them. They achieve this by including the same securities as a benchmark market index like the popular S&P 500 based on market cap size, avoiding the risks of picking individual stocks.

When you invest in an S&P 500 index fund, for example, you essentially invest a small amount into partial shares of the 500 large U.S. companies comprising that index in proportion with their size in the index. So if Apple stock makes up 5% of the index value, 5% of your index fund investment goes towards Apple.

As the market rises and falls, so does your index fund. You get both low expense ratios under 0.1% and instant diversification across key sectors rather than relying on just a few stocks performing.

Importantly, index funds don't require stock picking expertise to manage.

Why Invest in Index Funds?

Simplicity

Index funds provide an elegantly simple way to participate in market growth long term without worrying about losing on individual stock gambles or paying high fees for stock pickers' expertise. Just set and largely forget!

Diversification

Rather than putting all your eggs in a few baskets and hoping they perform well, index funds provide built-in diversification matching the market itself for lower volatility. They work excellently as foundational portfolio holdings balanced with other assets.

Low Cost

Since no pricey expert management needed, index fund expense ratios stay ultra low - most between

0.03% to 0.09% annually, compared with over 1% for actively managed mutual funds picking individual stocks. Less fees mean more investment returns in your pocket.

Compounding Growth

The power of compounding growth makes consistent long term market returns through index funds shine. Invest early and reinvest earnings, then give your money decades to work as returns pile up exponentially over time through the 8th wonder of the world.

To build starter index fund positions, platforms like Vanguard and Fidelity provide excellent options like VOO or FSKAX tracking top U.S. markets. Platforms like Wealthfront or Betterment allow fast, easy automated portfolio building using index funds matched to investor goals and risk tolerance too.

By keeping investments simple, diversified and low cost through index funds, it becomes much easier to stay invested through market volatility while compound interest works its magic long term.

Building a Stock Portfolio

Crafting a Custom Stock Portfolio: Strategies for Selections and Risk Management

Are you looking to tap into the wealth building potential of stock investing, but don't know where to begin in choosing companies? Crafting a well-balanced portfolio provides exposure to share in profits as companies grow. Blending research with risk management establishes a foundation to compound earnings through the long haul.

Defining Goals

First, clarify your purpose and timeline. Investing for retirement in 30 years varies hugely from saving for a house down payment in 5 years. Longer time horizons allow more aggressive growth stocks while short term savings favor stable assets. Your risk tolerance also determines suitable stock allocations.

Conservative investors stick near 30% while aggressive investors court above 60% stock holdings.

Sector Allocations

Historically over 90% of stock portfolio returns link to asset allocation more than individual stock-picking. Decide your broad exposure to major sectors like technology, healthcare, financials, communications, industrials, consumer staples/discretionaries. Index funds providing instant diversification are great for core holdings. For direct picks, choose leaders with staying power plus promising disrupters in key growth sectors like cloud computing, electric vehicles, or genomics.

Research Fundamentals

Mastering financial metric analysis lets you assess company health and valuation. Key indicators include consistent revenue and earnings growth, strong cash flow and manageable debt levels. Compare profitability margins and P/E ratios across industry peers. Favor durable competitive advantages with widening economic moats insulating profits long term.

Growth Stocks

Younger companies reinvesting profits to expand aggressively often see share prices rise exponentially in short periods. The tradeoff is higher volatility risk. Scrutinize disruptive models and leadership pedigree. Chase relative undervaluation, not overhyped momentum. Consider paring speculative growth stocks during market peaks while prices stay inflated.

Value Stocks

Established companies with strong fundamentals but trading below intrinsic value offer discounted opportunities less prone to manic swings. Look for turnaround narratives with improving margins and new efficiencies underway. Balance intrinsic value estimates against relative sector peer valuations.

Dividend Stocks

Mature companies rewarding investors through steady dividend payouts buffer against market drops. Seek out consistent dividend growers with healthy payout ratios below 60%. Reinvest dividend payments for compounding. Utilities, consumer staples and longstanding industrial giants offer classic dividend reliability.

Diversify Across Sectors

Mix choices across industry sectors and market cap size for portfolio stability as conditions affecting some companies lift others. Regularly rebalance positions back towards target allocations as valuations fluctuate to lock in gains.

Implement Loss Management

Market volatility tests even seasoned investors. Determine exit points beforehand for underperformers to prevent sinking into loss quicksand hoping in vain for rebounds. Set stop losses at 15-20% below purchase price. Reevaluate the bull case regularly and cut ties if fundamentals fade.

Invest Rolling Sums

Rather than attempting to time headlines, make consistent investments regardless of market drops or surges. Dollar cost averaging by passing recurring investments across varied market entry points smooths overall cost basis - harnessing bear drops to accumulate bargains while still steadily adding on upticks.

Allocate Patiently

Historically markets move upward over long arcs despite short-term storms. Maintain reasonable return expectations around 8-10% annualized averages for equity holdings left invested across decades not days. Let compounding work its magic through patient persistence meeting companies where they'll go rather than obsessing over erratic price charts.

Blend fundamentals-based analysis, risk management guardrails, and a long termcompound growth mindset to assemble a custom stock portfolio aligning your financial aspirations with companies poised to turn market-beating innovation into investor riches over the long haul. Stay diversified and consistent, letting time and compound gains overcome volatility on the journey to financial freedom.

Getting Started With Real Estate Investing

Real estate stands out as a powerful vehicle for building long-term wealth, with avenues to profit through appreciation and regular cash flow. However, the sheer size of properties as an asset class means you need significant capital to purchase investments directly. Excitingly, multiple paths now exist to participate in real estate with minimal upfront cash. By understanding options available today, new investors can craft a custom entry point aligning risk tolerances with reward potentials.

Let's explore popular strategies for getting started in real estate investing:

REITs

Real estate investment trusts aggregate funds from investors to assemble property portfolios, then pass a portion of profits directly through to shareholders. REITs trade publicly like stocks, providing instant diversification across larger commercial developments like apartment complexes, malls, warehouses and healthcare facilities. Investors benefit through steady dividends plus market price appreciation over time. Index funds containing REITs offer further diversification for those preferring passive vehicles.

Crowdfunding

Platforms like Fundrise reshaped real estate investing by allowing individuals to collectively fund vetted development projects for as little as $500. You browse investment choices online, then receive payouts as projects lease up or sell. Typical crowdfunded offerings include new construction financing, bridge loans to rehab neglected properties, and purchasing existing income-producing assets. Historically accessible only to the wealthy, crowdfunding opens real estate opportunities to all while still ensuring proper due diligence by experienced sponsors.

House Hacking

Among residential plays, "house hacking" provides an ingenious entry point requiring minimal cash. Investors purchase a small multifamily property, live in one unit personally, then rent the other unit(s) to cover or exceed the mortgage. Renter payments effectively eliminate housing costs for the owner while also forcing savings via principal paydown. After a few years, equity built plus rental income history aids financing larger acquisitions. House hacking works best in cash flow positive markets with solid rental demand.

BRRR Method

The "buy, rehab, rent, refinance, repeat" (BRRR) system follows a similar trajectory by leveraging sweat equity to build equity then scale. Investors purchase deteriorated properties well below market value, perform renovations boosting aesthetic appeal, quickly lease renovated units at top rents, then tap new equity through cash-out refinancing to repeat the process. Millionaires like Grant Cardone built entire empires this way despite limited initial capital.

Wholesaling

For the more sales inclined, wholesaling offers another fast-paced entry point. Investors scout underpriced or neglected properties in need of renovation, then contract to purchase them at deep discounts. Next, they market the deal with a marked up assigned contract to an end buyer who will actually complete renovations and rent or flip the home. The wholesaler pockets the difference while avoiding hands-on work. However, this high volume strategy relies heavily on marketing and negotiations skill.

Expanding into commercial investments like small multi-family complexes can also prove highly lucrative but involves greater upfront capital and specialized analytical knowledge. Those newer to real estate investing may prefer starting with more accessible entry points like REITs, crowdfunding or residential turnkey platforms. This allows you to learn ropes while building capital towards future larger plays.

Key Factors to Weigh

Each real estate investing strategy carries unique pros, cons and risk considerations. Assess options across these factors:

1. Needed Startup Capital - How much cash or financing required? What about ongoing reserves?

2. Hands-on Work Level - Will you self-manage or hire help? What are time requirements?

3. Income Stream Reliability - How consistent and passive is the cash flow?

4. Tax Advantages - Can you defer or exempt portions of investment gains?

5. Risk Management – How easy to diversify? How vulnerable to market swings?

6. Appreciation Potential - What timeframe to realize property value gains if selling?

7. Exit Strategy Flexibility - How easy to liquidate position when desired?

Analyzing across these comparative factors allows customizing your launch point to match personal objectives. Those desiring mostly passive income may prefer REITs or turnkey rentals. Folks open to some sweat equity can pursue BRRR or wholesaling flips. Regardless of chosen strategy, real estate investing rewards patience, analysis skills and long holding periods to realize full wealth building potential. But new flexible models offer viable ways to gain exposure without needing to directly buy whole buildings upfront.

In most industries, the barriers to profitable participation have lowered dramatically in recent decades. Real estate now follows suit through fractional ownership and collaborative funding models connecting viable deals to everyday investors on a broad scale for the first time. By starting small but starting now, you position yourself to compound modest initial capital over years through the immense wealth creation engine of property appreciation and rental income. Add in the tax advantages unique to real estate, and the horizons grow even brighter. It's an exciting time to tap into this historically privileged asset class now incrementally accessible to all.

CHAPTER 4

Accelerating with Leverage & Multiple Income Streams

Using business credit cards and financing

Beyond bootstrapping early operations on personal savings and credit cards, rapidly scaling ventures require capital influxes to seize growth opportunities before rivals. Business credit cards and financing provide fuel for expansion once revenue traction materializes. Used strategically, they empower scaling at velocity rates impossible when limited solely to internal cash flows.

Business Credit Cards

Once established for around one year, businesses can qualify for dedicated credit cards offering higher limits and bonus rewards tailored to common merchant expenses. Key perks include hefty signup bonuses, points or cashback on categories like advertising, shipping, office supplies, travel and fuel costs. These free up operating cash flows for other investments.

Ideal users consistently pay balances monthly, avoiding interest charges while benefiting from free float during grace periods. Such discipline plus reliable income streams establishes foundation for more flexible debt financing down the road.

Some personal liabilities remain with these cards, so start conservatively then request limit raises every 6 months supported by growing revenue streams reported on applications. Also, separate personal and business expenditure tracking helps optimize points and clearly deduct purchases come tax time.

Business Term Loans

Once beyond startup stage, term business loans allow accessing larger lump sums for major growth investments repaid in regular installments over fixed periods, usually between 1-5 years. Upfront capital injections fund large equipment purchases, real estate acquisition, new product manufacturing, digital marketing campaigns, inventory builds ahead of peak seasons and more.

Banks remain selective, preferring longstanding operations with high revenue, diverse income channels and hard assets for collateral. Newer funders like Credibly, Fundbox and Kabbage assess wider range of early stage ventures using quick online applications weighing total business performance rather than just personal credit scores.

Compare rates across multiple lenders as offers can vary widely. Avoid overextending with repayment periods beyond realistic income forecasts. The influx of capital invested wisely into amplified revenue engines should far outweigh loan repayment costs.

SBA Backed Lending

For eligible small businesses, SBA-backed bank loans provide attractive lower rate financing and longer repayment terms. Often used for commercial real estate purchasing or expansive new equipment, these loans encourage local economic development by guaranteeing a portion against bank's default risk, facilitating approvals.

R&D Tax Credits

Lesser known R&D tax credits offer lucrative opportunities, refunding up to 10% of annual research and development expenses for qualifying companies across nearly every industry. Many write off substantial investments as ordinary business costs without realizing they also qualify for substantial R&D tax credits. Accountants help document eligible activities like developing new technologies, systems, manufacturing processes, recipes, algorithms and even administrative workflow optimizations.

With the right foundations in place, creative financing strategies provide rocket fuel to accelerate ventures quickly seizing wide open markets. The key lies in deliberately channeling capital injections to magnify proven income generators already evidencing traction. Time properly leveraged financing to fund growth ambitiously while confidently maintaining healthy debt service coverage ratios. Move fast without reckless abandon by combining visionary boldness with financial judiciousness in deploying optimally structured capital towards your next breakthrough.

Building Business Systems and Teams

Scaling Up From Startup to Empire: Constructing Systems and Teams for Long Term Success

The early days of business often feel exhilarating yet wildly chaotic. Each order still provides a rush. New client meetings merit deep preparation and nervous energy to ensure flawless impressions. You personally juggle every task and relationship while continually putting out fires.

Then orders pick up. Clients expect more customization and reliable capacity. New opportunities demand exploration simultaneously across a dozen fronts. The overloaded lone wolf founder soon faces burnout, stagnating income and crumbling culture indicative of "the chaos stage" in small business development.

The best time to architect scalable systems? Before desperately needing them. By constructing organizational frameworks ready to absorb exponential growth early on, you preserve sanity while building capacity to handle volumes 100 even 1000X size over the startup phase. Here's how:

Design Ideal Client Journeys

Map exactly how customers will move through your sales process, onboarding, implementation, ongoing account management and follow up across timeframes. Engineer touchpoints to balance automation with human connection.

Document Core Processes

Detail every internal process required in managing accounts and delivering services. Identify pain points and improvement opportunities for smoother function. Update as enhancements develop, creating training manuals for new team members.

Assemble Complementary Teams

See hiring as a strategic capability investment, not just task coverage. Outline role requirements beyond immediate duties to include learning aptitudes as needs evolve. Assess candidates on cultural fit and work ethic in addition to base competencies - these become harder to instill later. Understand team dynamics scrubbing dysfunctions early. Institute quarterly reviews balancing appreciations of progress with developmental feedback tightening alignments.

Build Scalable Tech Infrastructure

Structure workflows around customer/team interface platforms creating centralized systems for institutional knowledge retention and access. Cloud-based services like GSuite, Trello, Slack, Intercom and Zapier connect previously siloed processes into seamless orchestrations. Automate repetitive tasks where possible to boost consistency and free up creative human efforts elsewhere.

Standardize Core Offerings

Balance tailoring services to client needs with the efficiency of packaged offerings pre-designed for common requests. Start with a few versatile building block products/programs that incorporate flexibility through modular add-ons and custom accents. Test reception continuously and expand options once uptake validates demand.

Create Feedback Loops

Listen voraciously to team insights and customer input. Build processes to quickly identity problems and implement changes. Idea collection boxes, regular quick surveys and lead user panels generate suggestions balancing early adopter desires against silent majority preferences to avoid over-customizing.

Set Proactive Milestone Goals

Look beyond handling day-to-day orders to project major scaling signposts. Set goals for team size, location expansion, client numbers, revenue milestones, new offerings. Connect hiring and operations expansion directly to benchmarks indicating infrastructure must grow to support next level. Make leveling up organizationally intrinsic to evolving rather than just trying to push existing structures past built capacities.

Culture Cultivation

Formalize rituals strengthening workplace culture and aligning people to purpose - the foundation uplifting companies as personalities supercharging productivity. Shared meals, volunteer days, celebratory traditions and offsite retreats build trust and belonging. Emphasize connection and contribution company-wide.

By building business bones ready for rapid fleshing, the pains of progress smooth into joyful expansion. Growth becomes deliberate extension of existing framework rather than crisis-driven makeshift pushes risking collapse. With robust systems for channeling rising tides into flowing momentum, breakthrough chasms transform into springboards. Ready yourself to scale mightily.

Acquiring Cash-Flowing Assets

The quest for true financial freedom eventually leads most investors towards prioritizing accumulation of cash-flowing assets - holdings like rental properties, dividends stocks, eCommerce stores or recurring-revenue businesses that reliably generate regular income only somewhat tied to ongoing work requirements.

The Appeal of Cash Flow

Cash-flowing assets provide stable passive income for compound growth while also typically appreciating over extended holding periods. This makes them ideal vehicles for diversifying income streams and accumulating long-term wealth.

For example, multi-family rental properties reliably collect monthly rents. Self-storage facilities only require occasional upkeep for continuous profits. A SaaS company structured around recurring subscriptions generates predictable revenue. In all cases, cash steadily flows whether you're actively working or not.

This allows investors to replace active income earned through trading hours for dollars with passive streams funding lifestyle desires. Substantial enough portfolios even fully cover living expenses so you needn't work for money at all unless by choice.

Acquisition Options

Many cash-flowing assets like commercial real estate require major capital to acquire outright. However, alternative investment platforms now provide fractionalized ownership opportunities to participate with smaller buy-ins through crowdfunding and REITs.

Beyond real estate, looking to small founder-run niche eCommerce stores and online services businesses offers accessible entry points to acquire entirely with potential for optimized growth leveraging digital capabilities once integrated into a larger portfolio.

Savvy investors seek out off-market deals before they hit listing sites through networked referrals and direct inquiry campaigns. Lead with win-win partnership messaging emphasizing synergies across operating entities and pooled resources realizing untapped potentials.

Implement Strategic Improvements

Once acquired, inject operating capital for strategic enhancements like refreshed branding and packaging, customer experience optimizations, expanded marketing channels, updated photography and sales copy, added team members, and new product or service development.

Improve tracking and analytics across marketing, sales funnels and fulfillment workflows. Test iterative changes quantifying impact on profitability and customer lifetime value. Invest net income into growth over taking heavy distributions during this customer acquisition and enhancement phase.

Reinvest for Compound Returns

Allow cash flow to compound over long holding periods instead of constantly trading into next ventures. Reinvest net revenues after operational costs to pay down debts expanding equity quicker. Refinance loans upon milestones to extract funds for additional acquisitions.

Duplicate what works across entities to rapidly compound equity and distributed income. Continuously funnel profits from mature assets into acquiring new positions.

By taking an ownership mindset and staying eager to learn, even first time investors can acquire simple small businesses built upon recurring revenue models or reliable rental income streams. Streamline operations for profit maximization then use consistent cash flow to acquire additional assets compounding portfolio equity. In time, even modest initial capital can snowball into impressive bounties of passive income generating true financial freedom.

CHAPTER 5

Wealth Creation for the Long-Term

Tax strategies as you scale

With dedication and wise investments, your assets begin accumulating at an accelerating rate over months and years. Yet without strategies protecting the fruits of your labor from disproportionate taxation, hard-earned capital dissipates quickly to government coffers. Proper tax planning becomes imperative to preserve and extend wealth for greater positive societal impact through philanthropy, your family legacy and business ventures uplifting communities.

The standard personal income tax rates up to 37% represent only initial leakages reduced through retirement accounts and other deferred strategies. But eventual withdrawals or asset sales trigger multiple layers of capital gains taxes, gift taxes, estate taxes and more dissipating 70 cents or more of every dollar moved. Even changing states adds tax residency complexities. Without advanced planning, wealth compounds far slower and distributes significantly less over time.

Sophisticated investors implement structures allowing more money remaining invested for further growth while controlling eventual tax hits. Major planning avenues to consider include:

Trusts and Family Entities

By transferring asset titles from personal names into various specialty entities, you dial in additional control over who receives distributions, how assets pass to future generations, and when tax consequences apply.

For example, domestic asset protection trusts help shield assets from creditors or lawsuits. Charitable remainder trusts allow selling assets tax-free and collecting residual payouts later. Irrevocable life insurance trusts exclude death benefit payouts from estates. Family limited partnerships consolidate investment entities under customized rules on distributions and succession structures.

Each structure carries unique tax implications when funded, dissolved or granted beneficiaries. Weighing options warrant sitting down with estate planning attorneys clarifying immediate and future needs.

Annual Gift Tax Exclusion

Currently, individuals can gift up to $16,000 value per year, per recipient free of lifetime gift and estate tax exemptions. Gifted amounts also shift future appreciation and income generation out of the estate.

Consider maxing annual family gifting while embedding assets into trusts triggering various tax savings down the road. This effectively layers tax strategies for optimal compounding and wealth shifting over decades.

Opportunity Zone Investing

The 2017 tax overhaul established "Opportunity Zones" - economically distressed areas offering new investments held over 5-7 years substantial tax reductions including: No tax on eventual capital gain appreciation, tax-free wealth shifting to heirs, and tax deductions reducing income tax.

When you sell highly-appreciated investments in the future, quickly redeploying proceeds into Opportunity Zone developments defers and reduces capital gains taxes owed while supporting community revitalization efforts in overlooked metros prime for growth.

Residence Planning

Given rising income and estate tax rates, declaring primary legal residence merits ongoing consideration. Florida and Texas levy no state income tax while Tennessee exempts certain dividend and interest income.

Meanwhile, living abroad substantially reduces investing reporting requirements and taxable holdings. Just spending enough days residing elsewhere may significantly reduce future tax exposure. Consult international tax specialists when assessing options.

Charitable Planning

Charitable trust structures provide major tax advantages while still directing wealth to causes important you. Charitable remainder trusts pay residual amounts to designated charities only after lifetime payouts to original asset contributors and/or their heirs.

Similarly, donor-advised funds allow maximizing deductions today while taking years to distribute to favorite nonprofit groups. Supporting personal passions while saving substantial sums remains achievable with planning.

In our uncertain political environment, tax regimes continue growing more punitive against high wealth individuals without contingencies in place. What constitutes aggressive planning versus unlawful evasion remains open to interpretation. Stay mindful of risks and consult experienced tax attorneys to ensure full compliance.

With the right education and structures aligned to your situation, sizable wealth compounds increasingly tax-free for lifetimes and generations down the road. Each strategy alone provides value – collectively, their benefits compound for substantial future-proofing of finances against excessive taxation. Take time now for wealth preservation as you work towards prosperity for the long run.

Setting Up Trusts and Legacy Planning

After decades accumulating valuable assets through entrepreneurial ventures, investments and real estate, the fruits of your labor now represent substantial wealth ready for transfer. Beyond securing your own comfortable retirement, you feel called to steward resources in empowering your family lineage across generations not just financially, but in character and purpose as well.

This noble intention reaches fulfillment through deliberate wealth structuring ahead of time for heirs still developing maturity and wisdom. By setting up trusts transferring oversight according to values-based principles, you ensure resources benefiting beloved descendants instead of derailing lives unprepared to constructively handle significant capital inflows.

While conveying confidence in capacities evolving over time, transferring lump sums into trusts enables installing thoughtful controls before absolving them feels prudent:

Incentive Trusts

Details conditions beneficiaries must meet for accessing portions of principal assets or income streams from trusts. These motivational milestones encourage developing wise money management, pursuing education, involving in philanthropy, maintaining family harmony, avoiding substance issues, preventing unwanted power struggles over resources, and contingently matching heirs' financial manifestations to your cellular-level life intentions for family members. Customize to nurture growth for unique personalities within bloodlines while upholding standards aligned with your wealth creation journey.

Dynasty Trusts

Established to exist and distribute assets beyond lifetimes of original grantors. Trust terms protect assets from divorces, bankruptcies, lawsuits and imprudent spending of heirs while minimizing estate taxes across generations. Specify succession structures over decades/centuries while infusing enduring family values and consensus around wealth stewardship.

Asset Protection Trusts

Designed to shelter property from existing/future claims of beneficiaries' creditors. May allow access only under strict trustee discretion preventing withdrawals even during financial duress scenarios like personal lawsuits, preventing forfeiture of nest eggs through no direct fault of heirs. Provide insulation against misjudgments available to be learned from without costing everything.

Testamentary Trusts

Outlined in your will to transfer into effect and distribute inheritance to designated beneficiaries after passing. Terms may direct layered payouts over time, concluding after predetermined ages allowing incremental rather than sudden capital access based on trustee assessment of evolving maturity demonstrated through adulthood.

No matter the income level, wise parents feel protective towards innocent children and young adults still navigating foundational life lessons. For financially successful patriarchs and matriarchs, that vigilance includes shielding heirs from heavy wealth itself until discernment catches up to net worth numbers.

By appointing trust executors to distribute resources deliberately when beneficiaries reach suitable maturity instead of limiting launch points for the next generation, lasting family legacies compound paying dividends for generations to come. Install those controls now through advanced planning to ensure your life's work finances vital impact rather than descent into excess and instability for loved ones.

CONCLUSION

There are clearly numerous methods for generating income online today to supplement or potentially replace a traditional job. From online freelancing platforms connecting independent professionals to remote opportunities at companies; to building passive income channels through affiliate marketing, dropshipping stores or information products - the possibilities span widely.

However with many competing options now saturating the work-from-home landscape, the most realistic, financially sustainable pursuits share a few common components. Identifying and developing an online money-making niche pertinent to your innate strengths and interests is key. This channels efforts efficiently while sustaining motivation longer-term - exponentially elevating success over time through experience.

Additionally, providing real value to others through products or services addressing genuine needs is indispensable. Whether solving problems, facilitating progress, informing decisions or simply entertaining - concentrating value sets profitable ventures apart from the masses of short-lived attempts. Building an engaged customer base grows more probable through repeat value delivery.

Embracing continual learning in our rapidly evolving online environment also cannot remain understated if one expects maintaining stable profits. Staying current with new technologies, software tools, changing algorithms and fresh competitor innovations greatly empowers strategy - allowing identification of new opportunities while mitigating redundancy and losing relevance. Stubbornly clinging to rigid concepts spells falling behind.

Patience and persistence through a reasonable ramp up period is equally vital until momentum gains traction. Sufficient trial and error is required for refining techniques, establishing authority, earning trust in unfamiliar markets and gradually increasing exposure. Financial growth generally compounds progress; overnight success is atypical despite exceptions.

By narrowing niche focus on high-value problems needing solutions, continually progressing skills and knowledge alongside market changes, persistently producing quality content that nurtures relationships, and allocating consistent effort over an adequate timespan - nearly anyone stands to profit handsomely online in some capacity today. The most sustainable and lucrative business models deliver authentic value above else. When helping enough people, achieving rewarding and flexible remote work must follow.

Disclaimer

Though, every illustrated technique/secret in this book were aimed to show its readers the hidden way to making wealth, the author holds no responsibility to any consequence upon their applications by the readers.

Till we meet at the top, I wish you peace and riches.

….. Godwins Inkline.